Exploring Caverns of Sonora

by Christine Griffith

PEARSON

Glenview, Illinois • Boston, Massachusetts
Chandler, Arizona • Upper Saddle River, New Jersey

Above the ground, Sonora looks like other places in Texas. But the amazing Caverns of Sonora are hidden just below the surface.

Beneath the Ground

Often, the most interesting things cannot be seen on the surface. When people explore below the surface, they can find amazing things.

On the surface, the land around Sonora, Texas, looks like many other places. Many farms and ranches are spread out over the area. However, beneath the surface, this area is very different.

One of the world's most beautiful *caverns* is just 150 feet below the ground. A cavern is an opening in the ground. It is big enough for people to go inside of.

---

surface: top part of something
explore: visit a new place to learn new things

Extend Language   Position Prepositions

We use special words to say where someone or something is. For example, *The book is <u>on</u> the desk.* These words are called position prepositions. Here are some of them:

at	between	on	below
next to	in	above	beneath
beside	inside of	under	

Can you find four position prepositions on this page?

The History of the Caverns of Sonora

In 1900, Stanley Mayfield owned a ranch near Sonora. One day, his dog chased a raccoon into a hole in the rocks. The hole was only about 20 inches wide. People did not know it then, but this was an amazing discovery. The dog discovered the Caverns of Sonora!

Over the next few years, people began to explore the cavern. However, they could go only about 500 feet inside the cavern. A giant *pit*, or hole, stopped them from going further. The explorers were careful. They needed to make sure no one plunged into the pit.

discovery: act of finding something before anyone else

At first, explorers could not get across this giant pit in the Caverns of Sonora.

The explorers could see things on the other side of the large pit. There were more *passageways*, or tunnels, in the rock. However, the explorers did not know how to get across the big pit.

In 1955, some *cavers*, or people who explore caverns, figured out how to get across the big pit. They crawled along a narrow ledge at the top of the cavern. Soon they saw many tunnels. The cavers saw something unusual in the new passageways. The passageways were filled with beautiful formations.

For a few years, only serious cavers went into the cavern. Then, in 1960, the cavern was open for everyone.

---

formations: shapes that have been made

The Caverns of Sonora have many passageways.

The Caverns of Sonora have many "rooms" that people have named. The caverns cover many miles.

The Caverns of Sonora stretch for miles. The unusual formations inside the caverns took thousands of years to be made. The formations are made of *minerals*. These natural materials are found in the ground. The minerals in the Caverns of Sonora formations are *crystals*, or rocks that shine and sparkle in the light.

The formations in the Caverns of Sonora have many shapes and sizes. Some of the formations look like other objects, so people have named them. For example, the caverns are home to formations called the Butterfly, angel's wings, and straws.

How the Caverns of Sonora Formed

Caverns are found in many different areas in the United States. They are found around the world too. These caverns form when rainwater moves through a special kind of rock called limestone.

Millions of years ago, a sea covered the area that is now Texas. Small animals lived in the sea. When these animals died, their bones and shells fell to the bottom. Over time, these bones and shells turned into limestone.

Later, Texas was no longer underwater. The Earth's surface moved and changed, but the layer of limestone stayed.

The land around Sonora, Texas, has a lot of limestone.

limestone

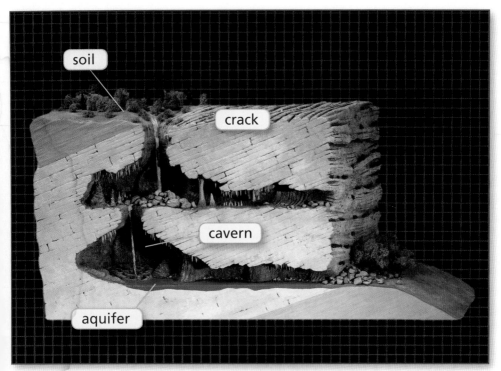

Rainwater moves through limestone and creates holes in the rock. Over many years, caverns form.

When it rained, the water moved through the soil and limestone rock on its way to the *aquifer*. An aquifer is an area underground that holds water.

As rainwater moved through small cracks in the limestone, the limestone **dissolved**. This made larger cracks in the limestone. More water moved through the limestone, which made the cracks bigger. Over time, these cracks slowly became caverns.

Caverns form very slowly. It can take more than 100,000 years for a cavern to form that is big enough for a person to crawl through.

---

dissolved: broke apart and got mixed into a liquid

stalactites

stalagmites

Cavern Formations

After the caverns were made, the beautiful crystal formations inside started forming. The Caverns of Sonora are still "growing" too. New mineral formations are being made right now. Many kinds of formations can be found in the caverns.

Stalactites

Stalactites are formations that hang from the top of a cavern. Water drips slowly down these formations. The water has minerals dissolved in it. Over time, the water leaves more minerals and the stalactites get bigger.

Stalagmites

Stalagmites are formations that start on the floor of a cavern and rise up. Stalagmites form when water drips from the top of the caverns.

Columns

Sometimes stalactites and stalagmites meet to form columns. These columns stretch from the floor to the *ceiling,* or the top of the cavern.

column

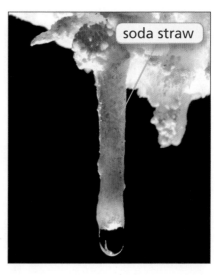

flowstone

Flowstone

A flowstone formation looks like a waterfall. It is made of hard minerals, not flowing water. Flowstone forms when water flows over parts of a cavern and leaves minerals behind.

Soda Straws

Soda straws look like straws you drink from. They are tubes that have air in the center. They grow longer over time because water drips down the inside of the straw. Then the water leaves more minerals at the end of the straw.

soda straw

9

helectites

Helectites

Helectites are formations that have a twisted shape. Some of the most famous formations in the Caverns of Sonora are helectites. They are made when wind in the caverns shape the mineral formations.

Cavern Explorers

Many people like to explore caverns. Today, people can see all the beauty of the Caverns of Sonora on a *tour*. A tour is a trip with a leader. The Caverns of Sonora have lights, paths, and stairs to help people stay safe inside the caverns.

Other people like to explore caverns by themselves. These people must be careful because caverns can be dangerous. People can get lost in the dark or stuck in small spaces. They can fall into deep holes.

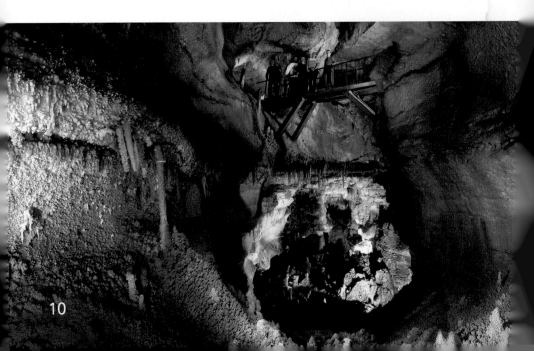

Cavers need the right equipment. Rocks sometimes fall inside caverns. So cavers must wear helmets. A helmet keeps a caver's head safe from the falling rocks.

Caverns are very dark inside, so cavers need to bring lights. Cavers usually wear lights on their helmets called headlamps. This way, they do not have to carry lights with their hands. They can use their hands for crawling and climbing.

Cavers often need to crawl through small passageways. They wear gloves to keep their hands safe. They also wear pants and special pads to keep their knees and elbows safe.

In some caverns, cavers need to climb into or out of pits. These cavers need rope and special skills.

---

equipment: clothing and tools to do a job

headlamp

helmet

gloves

Cavers need the right equipment to stay safe.

Rules for Safe Caving

- Never go caving alone.
- Stay with your group.
- Plan your trip carefully.
- Tell someone your plans.
- Have the right equipment.
- Do not do anything that is unsafe.

Protecting Caverns

Every year, thousands of people visit the Caverns of Sonora. They go to see the caverns' beautiful formations. However, caverns are *fragile*. Things that are fragile can easily break or be harmed.

Caverns are natural wonders. They show us a lot about changes to the Earth over time. It is fun to visit caverns, but people must be careful to protect the caverns. Never leave garbage in caverns, and never break off any pieces of formations. This way, everyone can enjoy caverns for many years.

before

after

These photos show a famous formation called the Butterfly in the Caverns of Sonora. In 2006, someone broke off and stole one of the Butterfly's wings.